Dogfulness

Dogfulness

The Path to Inner Peace

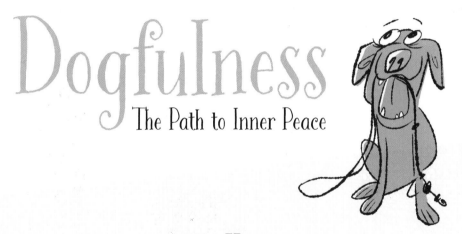

Andrews McMeel Publishing®

Kansas City · Sydney · London

Andrews McMeel Publishing, LLC
an Andrews McMeel Universal company
1130 Walnut Street, Kansas City, Missouri 64106
www.andrewsmcmeel.com

15 16 17 18 19 TEN 10 9 8 7 6 5 4 3 2 1

ISBN: 978-1-4494-7240-5

Library of Congress Control Number: 2015940897

Compiled *Michael Powell*
Illustrations *Lorenzo Montatore*
Design *Milestone Design*

ATTENTION: SCHOOLS AND BUSINESSES
Andrews McMeel books are available at
quantity discounts with bulk purchase for
educational, business, or sales promotional use.
For information, please e-mail the Andrews
McMeel Publishing Special Sales Department:
specialsales@amuniversal.com.

Something important is spreading throughout the world: More and more people are discovering the amazing power of dogfulness.

Inside this book, dozens of canny canines reveal the secret to living more dogfully.

At home, at work, on the sofa, or lying curled up under the kitchen table, being dogful is the way to be.

Restore your attention or bring it to a new level by dramatically slowing down whatever you're doing.

Sharon Salzberg

Take a **walk outside**—
it will serve you far more
than pacing around
in your mind.

Rasheed Ogunlaru

The Path to Inner Peace

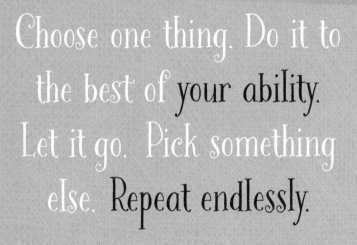

Choose one thing. Do it to the best of your ability. Let it go. Pick something else. Repeat endlessly.

Lionel Fisher

Rest is not idleness, and to lie sometimes on the grass under the trees on a summer's day, listening to the murmur of water, or watching the clouds float across the blue sky, is by no means a waste of time.

John Lubbock

The Path to Inner Peace

Running is about more than just putting one foot in front of the other; it is about our lifestyle and who we are.

Joan Benoit Samuelson

The greatest gift you can give
(yourself or anyone else)
is just being present.

Rasheed Ogunlaru

To travel hopefully is a better thing than to arrive.

Robert Louis Stevenson

You make your
own happiness.

Harold Klemp

The Path to Inner Peace

No act of kindness,
no matter how small,
is ever wasted.

Aesop

Amidst the worldly comings and goings, observe how endings become beginnings.

Tao Te Ching

The Path to Inner Peace

Walk as if you are
kissing the Earth
with your feet.

Thich Nhat Hanh

Persistence and determination are always rewarded.

Christine Rice

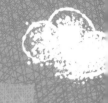

Don't deal bitterly with the enemy you see. Deal with the greater enemy that sent your enemy to you.

Israelmore Ayivor

The greatest step
towards a life
of simplicity is to
learn to let go.

Steve Maraboli

The Path to Inner Peace

There is a time for many words, and there is a time for sleep.

Homer

Perseverance
is failing nineteen times
and succeeding the
twentieth.

Dr. J. Andrews

The Path to Inner Peace

Everything is meant to be lost, that the soul may stand in unhampered nothingness.

Meister Eckhart

Thou canst not travel
on the Path before
thou hast become
that Path itself.

Helena Petrovna Blavatsky

Love only grows by sharing,
and the only way you can have
any more love for yourself
is by giving it away.

Brian Tracy

What you do not want
done to yourself,
do not do to others.

Confucius

In the end, these things matter most: How well did you love? How fully did you live? How deeply did you learn to let go?

Jack Kornfield

We are never more fully alive,
more completely ourselves,
or more deeply engrossed in
anything, than when
we are at play.

Charles E. Schaefer

It is good to collect things, but it is better to go on walks.

Anatole France

A barrier is of ideas, not of things.

Mark Caine

The Path to Inner Peace

When you realize how perfect everything is you will tilt your head back and laugh at the sky.

Attributed to Buddha

Treasure your
relationships, not
your possessions.

Anthony J. D'Angelo

Do one thing every day that scares you.

Mary Schmich

Until we can receive
with an open heart, we
are never really giving
with an open heart.

Brené Brown

Water is the driving force of all nature.

Leonardo da Vinci

Be an **independent** thinker at all times, and ignore anyone who attempts to **define** you in a limiting way.

Sherry Argov

Alone we can do so little; together we can do so much.

Helen Keller

Just watch this moment, without trying to change it at all. What is happening? What do you feel? What do you see? What do you hear?

Jon Kabat-Zinn

The Path to Inner Peace

Never curse a fall.
The ground is where
humility lives.

Yasmin Mogahed

The only true
thing is what's
in front of you
right now.

Ramona Ausubel

This too shall pass.

Attar of Nishapur

When you really like
someone, tell them.
Sometimes you only
get one chance.

H. Jackson Brown Jr.

The Path to Inner Peace

Sometimes opportunities float right past your nose. Work hard, apply yourself, and be ready. When an opportunity comes you can grab it.

Julie Andrews

If everyone started off the day singing, just think how happy they'd be.

Lauren Myracle

There's never enough
of the stuff you
can't get enough of.

Patrick H. T. Doyle

A leader takes people where
they want to go. A great leader
takes people where they don't
necessarily want to go,
but ought to be.

Rosalynn Carter

Your body is
not a temple, it's an
amusement park.
Enjoy the ride.

Anthony Bourdain

There are so many more important things to worry about than how you're perceived by strangers.

Dennis Lehane

Simplicity
is ultimately a
matter of focus.

Ann Voskamp

Shame is always easier to handle if you have someone to share it with.

Craig Thompson

94

When you have an intense contact of love with nature or another human being, like a spark, then you understand that there is no time and that everything is eternal.

Paulo Coelho